Kalaupapa

A Portrait

Photographs by Wayne Levin

Text by Anwei Skinsnes Law

Arizona Memorial Museum Association + *Bishop Museum Press*

Bishop Museum Special Publication Number 91

NOTE: *Unless otherwise indicated, the photographs that appear in these pages are by Wayne Levin and are from his personal collection.*

First published in 1989
Arizona Memorial Museum Association, Honolulu, Hawaiʻi
Ansil L. Saunders, President
Bishop Museum Press, Honolulu, Hawaiʻi
W. Donald Duckworth, Director, Bishop Museum

Edited by Nelson Foster
Designed by Barbara Pope

LIBRARY OF CONGRESS CATALOG CARD NO. 89–62–469
ISBN 0–930897–45–5

TITLE PAGE: *The north shore of Molokaʻi as seen from the graveyard of St. Philomena Church, 1986*

Kalaupapa viewed from Pala'au State Park, 1985.

FOREWORD

WHEN I FIRST met Wayne Levin, we discussed the need to record Kalaupapa on film before the settlement, as many of us know it, was gone. I noted that the photographs might not be published or fully appreciated for many years to come but that it was, nevertheless, important that this phase of Kalaupapa's history be documented as soon as possible. Recognizing both these facts, Wayne undertook not only to photograph the settlement but also to capture its spirit—the loneliness, the dignity, the aloha. Through his photographs, he has given us and future generations a means by which to remember this unique community and its place in world affairs.

Anwei Skinsnes first visited Kalaupapa more than twenty years ago and, when it became a national historical park, was among the first to argue that the Park Service needed to do more than simply preserve the physical remains of the settlement. She recognized that it was essential that the human story be told, and in the ensuing years, with our support, she recorded over one hundred hours of oral history from Kalaupapa residents and other key individuals. Many of the quotations that accompany Wayne's photographs have been excerpted from this material.

The National Park Service is pleased that, through the Arizona Memorial Museum Association, it has been able to assist Wayne and Anwei to realize their dream of publishing this book. We are especially happy that it is being released in 1989, on the centennial of Father Damien's death, for it has enabled all of us involved to carry on his legacy by helping to improve understanding of Kalaupapa and its people.

Henry G. Law
First Superintendent
Kalaupapa National Historical Park

Wayne at Kalaupapa, 1986. Mary Belanger. Collection of Wayne Levin.

PREFACE

IN 1983, a friend who had recently visited Kalaupapa suggested that I photograph the Hansen's Disease settlement there. Realizing the importance of documenting this historic community and its last inhabitants, I made eighteen trips to Kalaupapa during the next three years, each time staying from three to seven days. This book is the result.

On my first trip, I carried a 35-millimeter camera, which is the equipment generally preferred for a project of this kind, but the photographs I brought back did not capture the spirit of the settlement to my satisfaction. Thereafter I used a 4 x 5 view camera, not so much for the fine detail provided by the larger film but because it forced me to slow down to Kalaupapa time. The deliberate pace necessitated by the large-format camera helped me enter the rhythm of Kalaupapa, which is much more like a small town of the past than like modern Honolulu, only twenty minutes away by light plane.

There were other barriers to overcome as well. I had been preceded by several photographers and journalists who had visited the peninsula briefly and published sensationalized views of the settlement and its people. Residents felt used and were understandably suspicious of yet another outsider intent on portraying them. It took time to win the trust that I needed to take their pictures. A good portrait always requires the cooperation of its subject, but in this case the requirement was explicit and legal. State law and Department of Health regulations for Kalaupapa stipulate that patients must give written permission before they may be photographed.

While this provision protects residents' privacy, especially from the cameras of unthinking tourists, it also perpetuates the stigma of Hansen's Disease by implying that there is something shameful about having it and continues a long history of paternalism. The people of Kalaupapa, as I know them, are proud survivors of an extraordinary injustice and are fully prepared to defend their own rights. They have a deeply significant story to tell and deserve to be seen and heard, not hidden away any longer. I have tried to serve as a vehicle for their story and to depict them with the dignity they merit.

Staying at Kalaupapa, one feels its isolation more keenly than a casual visitor is likely to. One day, walking beneath the two-thousand-foot cliffs that separate the peninsula from the rest of the island—"topside Moloka'i," as residents call it—I glimpsed tiny figures on the precipice above and suddenly had an overwhelming sense of my remoteness from the rest of the human race. It was like peering up from an unimaginably deep well. No doubt what I experienced was only a hint of what people felt when they were sentenced to spend the remainder of their years there.

Other eerie and poignant intimations of that life came as I explored the abandoned houses of the settlement. Vegetation is fast overtaking the many buildings that have fallen into disuse, but again and again the objects left behind—chairs, utensils, old clothes, calendars open to telltale dates—removed me from my easy present and offered me a powerful sense of the people who once dwelled there.

These days, of course, no one is compelled to live at Kalaupapa, and the settlement population is gradually diminishing. Cars that once crowded the streets are deteriorating along the shoreline, some of them already reduced to bits of rust scarcely discernible from the pebbles. Kalaupapa's days as an active settlement are numbered, and nature seems eager to reclaim the place even before its history is complete. This means the end of a way of life for its residents, and the change comes hard.

Fortunately, the National Park Service will succeed in saving Kalaupapa's key buildings and is working energetically to document the human drama that unfolded there and to convey it to visitors. While the ambience of the old settlement, with all its pathos, can never be fully restored, a sense of the drama and of the people who lived it will be preserved through oral histories, videotapes, and projects such as this. I feel privileged to have met and photographed the last residents of Kalaupapa, and I see this as their book, a testament to them and others now gone.

I hope the book will also help our society learn to fight its hysterical fear of poorly understood diseases. The need to publicize Kalaupapa's history and keep its lesson alive was brought home to me with new urgency in November 1986, when I showed some of these pictures in San Francisco at a conference of the Society for Photographic Education. The following day, Californians would go to the polls to vote on a proposition requiring forced quarantine of all AIDS patients.

That misguided initiative was soundly defeated, but other events make it plain that many people are as fearful today—as ready to ostracize a suffering minority—as they were 120 years ago in Hawai'i. A society so quick to deny the rights and even the humanity of the ill can hardly describe itself as just or decent. I hope this book will, in some small measure, hasten the day when the lesson of Kalaupapa will be understood at last.

☩   ☩   ☩

I OWE THANKS, first and foremost, to the many residents of Kalaupapa who shared their memories with me, guided me, extended hospitality, and in other ways made my visits to their hometown pleasant and productive. I cannot mention each one by name here, but I want to note with special appreciation the help I received from Henry Nalaielua, Bernard K. Punikai'a, Clarence Naia, Lucy Kaona, and the late John Kaona.

I am indebted to Mary Ellen Sorenson, who first suggested that I do a photographic study of Kalaupapa, and to the people and institutions whose support made both the study and this book possible: Gary Beito and the Arizona Memorial Museum Association, Henry Law and the National Park Service, the Kalaupapa Historical Society, and my collaborator Anwei Skinsnes Law. I am grateful to each of them for contributing not only to this effort but also to the larger project of keeping the legacy of Kalaupapa alive.

A word of special thanks also to Irene Letoto of the Damien Museum and Lynn Davis of Bishop Museum for helping us locate and publish historical photographs from the collections they oversee. We are especially honored that the Damien Museum has allowed us to publish images taken in the late 1800s by Kalaupapa physician Sidney Bourne Swift, including poignant scenes of Father Damien's last days. Honolulu photographer Bruce Erickson did an expert job of printing Dr. Swift's pictures from original glass plate negatives, which the Damien Museum recovered in a trunk of Father Damien's possessions that has been lost for nearly a century.

As these acknowledgments ought to make clear, the book in your hands is the product of considerable good fortune, trust, kindness, and cooperation. I am proud and grateful to have been a part of it.

Wayne Levin

Portrait of a patient, Kalaupapa, c. 1915. Unidentified photographer. Collection of the Damien Museum.

A Triumph of Spirit

IN THE ONE HUNDRED AND FIFTY years that leprosy has been known to Hawai'i, it has played a significant role in the islands' history, a role that has been overlooked in all but a few modern accounts. Far more than a medical problem, leprosy in Hawai'i has had social, religious, and political dimensions, and the debate about its treatment has encompassed the whole of island society. Cases appeared in the royal family and in the religious and medical communities, as well as among less privileged citizens.

In all, some eight thousand people were torn from their families and friends and exiled to a beautiful peninsula on the north coast of Moloka'i now known as Kalaupapa but properly called Makanalua. Surrounded by steep cliffs and rugged seas, the peninsula has the features of a natural prison and quickly gained a reputation as a "living tomb."

At the time they were confined at the Kalaupapa Settlement, the patients had no reason to believe that people of other places or of future generations would know or care what happened there, but from the start, the saga of Kalaupapa and its people has struck the hearts and minds of those who heard it. The story of Kalaupapa has been recounted by famous writers, including Charles Warren Stoddard, Robert Louis Stevenson, and Jack London, and has commanded the attention of statesmen like Theodore Roosevelt and Mahatma Gandhi.

The heroism of Father Damien DeVeuster, who devoted his life to the people of Kalaupapa, has particularly inspired the world community. His statue stands before the Hawai'i State Capitol and represents the islands in Statuary Hall in the United States Capitol, and together with his less famous colleague Mother Marianne Cope, Father Damien is now a candidate for canonization by the Catholic Church. The annals of health care also recognize a multitude of contributions that Hawai'i has made to both the medical and social treatment of leprosy.

Kalaupapa's designation as a national historical park on December 22, 1980, was an official recognition of the importance of Kalaupapa's history to Hawai'i, the nation, and the world. Still in its formative years, Kalaupapa National Historical Park is committed to the past, the present, and the future. It is dedicated to preserving memories of the past in order that valuable lessons might be learned from them. It is dedicated to protecting and maintaining the remaining community, ensuring that the present residents of Kalaupapa Settlement

Portrait of a patient, Kalaupapa, c. 1915. Unidentified photographer.
Collection of the Damien Museum.

I have seen sights that cannot be told, and heard stories that cannot
be repeated: yet I have never admired my poor race so much nor
(strange as it may seem) loved life more than in the settlement.

Robert Louis Stevenson

from *The Letters of Robert Louis Stevenson*

Young patient, Kalaupapa, date unknown.
Unidentified photographer. Collection of A. Law.

may live out their lives in this, their home. And it is dedicated to educating present and future generations about a disease that has been shrouded in fear and ignorance for centuries.

Historical Background[1]

Leprosy's origins in the islands can be traced to several well-documented cases noted among the Hawaiians in the 1830s. The most widely accepted theory is that leprosy was introduced by Chinese immigrants who were brought to Hawai'i to work as indentured laborers. The disease came to be known by two names, *ma'i pake* (the Chinese sickness) and *ma'i ali'i* (the royal sickness), the latter term indicating its incidence among and association with the Hawaiian royalty.

Reports of the disease grew in frequency during the 1850s, and by the following decade, expressions of concern and alarm echoed throughout the Hawaiian Kingdom. The disease became an official matter on January 3, 1865, when King Kamehameha V signed an "Act to Prevent the Spread of Leprosy." This law authorized the government to set aside land for the isolation of any person who might spread the disease if left "at large." After much discussion, it was decided to establish both a hospital for treatment of mild cases near the seashore in Honolulu and a settlement for advanced cases on the island of Moloka'i. Kalihi Hospital in Honolulu opened first, with forty-three persons admitted for treatment on November 13, 1865. Two months later, on January 6, the first "shipment" of patients was made to Kalawao, on the eastern side of Makanalua peninsula.

The peninsula has three traditional land divisions (*ahupua'a*)—Kalawao, Makanalua, and Kalaupapa—with the distance between Kalawao on the east and Kalaupapa on the west being about two and a half miles. In 1866, the Kalaupapa area was still in use as a Hawaiian fishing village, so Kalawao was selected as the site for the first leprosy settlement. Nearly thirty years later, in January of 1895, the last of Kalaupapa's original residents were forced to leave, and the settlement was increasingly concentrated on that more temperate side of the peninsula.

Conditions at the settlement were a constant source of controversy. Food and shelter were inadequate, and no physician could be found to reside there until 1879. Visiting doctors reportedly treated patients from afar, probing them with ten-foot-long poles and depositing medicines on a gate post to avoid direct contact. Feeling they had been abandoned in Kalawao to die, many patients saw no reason to abide by any rules. For many years, a state of lawlessness prevailed, with the strong dominating the weak and those

Settlement patients, c. 1910. Unidentified photographer. Collection of Bishop Museum.

Kalaupapa residents, c. 1915. Unidentified photographer. Collection of the Damien Museum.

whose leprosy was very advanced at the mercy of those whose illness was still in its early stages.

Tales of the settlement that circulated in Honolulu were full of drunkenness and debauchery, but not all the patients fit this image. Indeed, the beginnings of a church were established at Kalawao during the first year of the settlement, and members of its congregation later sought help in the construction of a proper church edifice. "You must not think that all of us are living in sin and degradation," they wrote in their appeal. "That is not so. Our greatest longing is to make a memorial to God here."[2] These prayers were answered when Siloama Congregational Church, "The Church of the Healing Spring," was consecrated on October 28, 1871. The following year, Brother Victorin Bertrant had a wooden

Ancient stone walls, Makanalua, 1984.

Kalawao Settlement, c. 1884. Photographer unknown. Collection of the Hawai'i State Archives. Siloama Church (left) would be rebuilt in 1885, its orientation rotated ninety degrees. St. Philomena Church, with a new nave and steeple added by Father Damien, is visible to the rear of Siloama.

chapel built in Honolulu and transported in segments to Kalawao, where it was blessed on May 30, 1872. This second church, dedicated to St. Philomena, would later be expanded by Father Damien and become widely known as "Father Damien's Church."

Eventually a Mormon church was also established at Kalawao. Jonathan H. Napela, a native Hawaiian who had been ordained a Mormon elder in 1870, accompanied his sick wife to Kalaupapa in 1873 and thereafter conducted services regularly. He was one of many who did not have leprosy but went to the settlement with their spouses, children, or parents and served as *kokua* (helpers).

Despite the presence of the churches and some improvements by the Board of Health, including construction of a hospital in 1867, law and order could not be maintained.

St. Philomena Church, Kalawao, c. 1890. Sidney Bourne Swift, M.D. Collection of the Damien Museum.

Patients committed crimes without fear of punishment, for no punishment could be worse than that which society had already dealt them. The troublemakers may have constituted only a minority, but it was they who dominated the settlement. Thus, the cry emanating from Kalawao was " *'A'ole kānāwai ma keia wahi*" — "In this place there is no law."[3] As horrible tales of Kalawao spread throughout the islands, families hid members who contracted leprosy, with the result that the disease continued to spread.

By 1873, when the young Belgian priest Father Damien arrived at the settlement, leprosy was no longer regarded in Hawai'i as a disease to be treated in a hospital by a doctor. It had become a crime. Having the disease was grounds for arrest; punishment was exile to Kalawao; and patients were condemned to survive as best they could with whatever aid the Board of Health felt able to provide. That same year, a concerted effort was made

St. Philomena Church, Kalawao, 11 July 1905. Alonzo Gartley. Collection of Bishop Museum.

to round up anyone suspected of having the disease, and attempts were made to enforce the Territory's segregation laws more strictly than in the past.

Prominent members of the *haole* (Caucasian) community publicly declared that leprosy was caused by licentiousness, with a few going so far as to reckon it the fourth stage of syphilis. Such proclamations were made in the implicit belief that leprosy was a native disease, one which no upright *haole* would contract. These beliefs were shattered in later years as members of the *haole*, Chinese, Japanese, and Filipino communities increasingly contracted the disease, but in the nineteenth century, leprosy primarily affected Hawaiians, owing to their poorly developed immune systems, their lack of preconceptions about the disease, and their belief that the sick should be cared for at home, not abandoned in some remote location.

Fervent calls for the isolation of people with leprosy were issued for the supposed good of the Hawaiian nation. At an extremely emotional meeting on June 10, 1873, the *haole*-led Hawaiian Evangelical Association drafted a document stating that segregation was the will of God and that it was the Association's duty to help the public realize this fact. Isolation of the sick was the only salvation for the Hawaiian people, the argument continued, and without it Hawai'i would degenerate into a "nation of lepers." The report went on to ask: "Do we consider what this means? It means the disorganization and total destruction of civilization, property values, and industry, of our churches, our contributions, our Hawaiian Board and its work of Missions. It means shame, defeat, and disgraceful overthrow to all that is promising and fair in the nation."[4]

At the time this statement was made, Father Damien had been living at Kalawao for exactly one month. To him, it was irrelevant whether leprosy's spread affected property values or contributions to the Missions; he concerned himself with the effect that leprosy had on the individual. While others made loud pronouncements about what *should* be done for the good of society, Father Damien concentrated on what *had* to be done for the individual who had been removed from his home in order to protect society. Unwilling to watch the patients sit waiting to die, Father Damien enlisted their help in numerous projects. Together they built houses, improved the water supply, and planted fruit trees.

Damien's practical nature and fluent use of Hawaiian led the patients to regard him differently from the white men who had come before. He helped them all, Catholic and non-Catholic alike, and always attempted to make them feel comfortable and accepted. Most important, the patients found in him someone who genuinely cared about them, and they, in turn, began to care about themselves and about each other.

Charles Warren Stoddard, professor of literature at the University of Notre Dame, visited Kalawao in 1884 and was one of the few to write about Father Damien on the basis of firsthand observations. "His cassock was worn and faded," Stoddard wrote, "his hair tumbled like a school-boy's, his hands stained and hardened by toil; but the glow of health was in his face, the buoyancy of youth in his manner; while his ringing laugh, his ready sympathy, and his inspiring magnetism told of one who in any sphere might do a noble work, and who in that which he has chosen is doing the noblest of all works. This was Father Damien."[5]

While Father Damien served the immediate needs of Kalawao residents, scientists in Honolulu and around the world pursued a search for a cure. The same year that Father Damien arrived at the settlement, Dr. Gerhard Hansen of Norway discovered the leprosy

Father Damien with girls of the settlement, c. 1880. Unidentified photographer. Collection of the Hawai'i State Archives.

bacillus or, as he called it, the *"Bacillus leprae,"* a breakthrough that revolutionized leprosy research. Dr. Hansen's discovery disproved the theory that leprosy was hereditary and focused future research on its nature as an infectious disease and on its potential cure. Though research was actively carried out in Norway, in Hawai'i, and elsewhere, three decades would pass before even a prospective remedy, chaulmoogra oil, was found, and an effective cure, the sulfone drugs, would not be discovered until the 1940s.

In the meantime, the Hawai'i Territorial Board of Health received numerous petitions from unlicensed physicians and laypeople who claimed they could cure leprosy. The Board permitted some of these purported healers to try their cures, thereby establishing a trend toward lax medical standards for treatment of leprosy.

Denied hope by the medical community, people with leprosy looked to the churches for salvation—if not in this life, then in the next. Besides Father Damien, there were others who answered this call and devoted their lives to the care of patients at the settlement. Among these religious workers, Mother Marianne Cope and Brother Joseph Dutton stand out for their long and ardent service.

Mother Marianne Cope came to Hawai'i in 1883 to work at the Kaka'ako Branch Hospital, which had opened two years before and served as Honolulu's primary leprosy facility.[6] In 1888, she moved to the settlement with Sisters Leopoldina Burns and Vincentia McCormick to run the Bishop Home for girls, established that same year on the Kalaupapa side of the peninsula. Father Damien had been officially diagnosed as having leprosy in 1885, and the three sisters' arrival gave him assurance that his work would be continued and "his children" would not be forgotten. He was especially pleased to have the sisters come because he had long recognized a need for women's assistance in caring for the residents, particularly unaccompanied youngsters.

An outstanding administrator, nurse, and pharmacist, Mother Marianne served leprosy patients in Hawai'i for thirty-five years, yet her name is little known, and the magnitude and importance of her contribution to treatment of leprosy has gone largely unrecognized. Her relative anonymity stems primarily from her practice of shunning personal publicity in order to direct attention to her work. Believing it essential that the patients lead rich and full lives, she made sure that those under her care had meaningful daily contact and encouraged them to live and die with dignity. A century later, this philosophy of maintaining patients' personal dignity in the face of death has become the foundation of the hospice movement and similar efforts to support the terminally ill.

When Robert Louis Stevenson traveled to Kalaupapa in 1889, he spent many long hours with Mother Marianne. Captivated by her gentle spirit and devotion to the patients, he composed a poem dedicated to her:

> To see the infinite pity of this place,
> The mangled limb, the devastated face,
> The innocent sufferers smiling at the rod,
> A fool were tempted to deny his God.
>
> He sees; he shrinks; but if he look again,
> Lo, beauty springing from the breast of pain!—
> He marks the sisters on the painful shores,
> And even a fool is silent and adores.[7]

In contrast to Mother Marianne, who worked in silence, was Brother Dutton, who came to the settlement to assist Father Damien in July of 1886. Forty-three years later, Dutton recalled his arrival:

> Father Damien was there from Kalawao with his buggy—low, wide, rattling—and a steady old horse. I introduced myself as coming with King Kalakaua's permission. . . . We climbed into the old buggy and were off for Kalawao. . . .
>
> . . . I was happy as we drove over that morning. The Father talked eagerly, telling how he had wanted Brothers here, but the Mission had none to spare yet. So he called me Brother, as I had come to stay. . . . He was full of plans that morning . . . the dreams he had always had.[8]

Dutton's arrival coincided with Father Damien's realization that his days were numbered.

Brother Dutton in his office with boys from Baldwin Home, Kalawao, date unknown.
Unidentified photographer. Collection of the Hawai'i State Archives.

Filled with ideas and plans, the priest anxiously started new projects and often left them for his lay associate to finish.

Father Damien's illness worsened gradually until, in March of 1889, he became too weak to work. "He lay for three weeks in the last stages, unable to say Mass, much of the time quite helpless . . . ," Dutton reported afterward. "In the last period of three weeks the disease, thus far very pronounced in outward manifestation, almost entirely left the surface, retreating, or I might say, advancing to the interior for the last attack, and ravaged in a fearful manner the throat, lungs, stomach, etc."[9] Despite intense pain, Father Damien was cheerful two weeks before his death, commenting, "How good God is, to have made me live long enough to see at this moment two priests at my side and the Franciscan Sisters at the Settlement! . . . I am no longer necessary; I am going to Heaven."[10] Perhaps he permitted the settlement's resident physician to photograph him in his deathbed as a testament to what his fellow sufferers had endured.

After Father Damien's death, many expected interest in the settlement to subside, but this did not occur, largely due to Brother Dutton's voluminous correspondence. His address book contained over four thousand names, and his mail sometimes weighed as much as fifty pounds. Dutton's letters, scattered in archives and personal collections throughout the United States, now provide valuable insights into life at the settlement.

Dutton initially went to the settlement to do penance and atone for what he felt had been a "degenerate decade" in his life, during which he had drunk more than his share of whiskey. He remained at the settlement for forty-four years. Honored for his work there by Theodore Roosevelt, Calvin Coolidge, Warren Harding, and Franklin Delano Roosevelt, Dutton possessed a colorful personality which helped to ensure that people remembered the settlement, its patients, and Dutton himself. Indeed, an elementary school in Beloit, Wisconsin, now bears his name, and a church in Stowe, Vermont, is dedicated to him and has murals of Damien, Dutton, and the sisters painted on its external walls.

Dutton's life has served as an inspiration to many because it carries with it a message, best expressed by Dutton himself. Over the years, many people wrote him to ask if they could assist him at the settlement, thinking it would be the perfect place to better themselves and find their life's work. To these inquiries Dutton replied: "I wish to guard you against having too high an estimate of the work here. Work performed with a good intention to accomplish the Will of Almighty God, for his Glory, is the same in one place as another. One's Molokai can be anywhere."[11]

✚   ✚   ✚

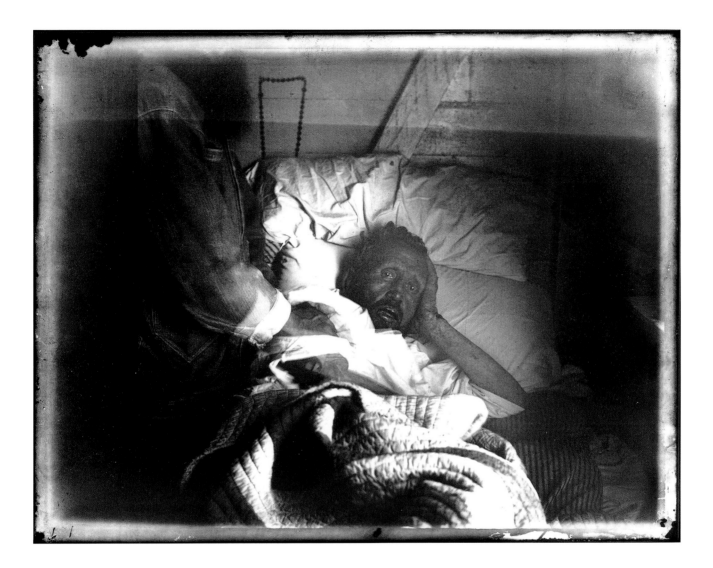

Father Damien the day before his death, Kalaupapa, 14 April 1889. Sidney Bourne Swift, M.D. Collection of the Damien Museum.

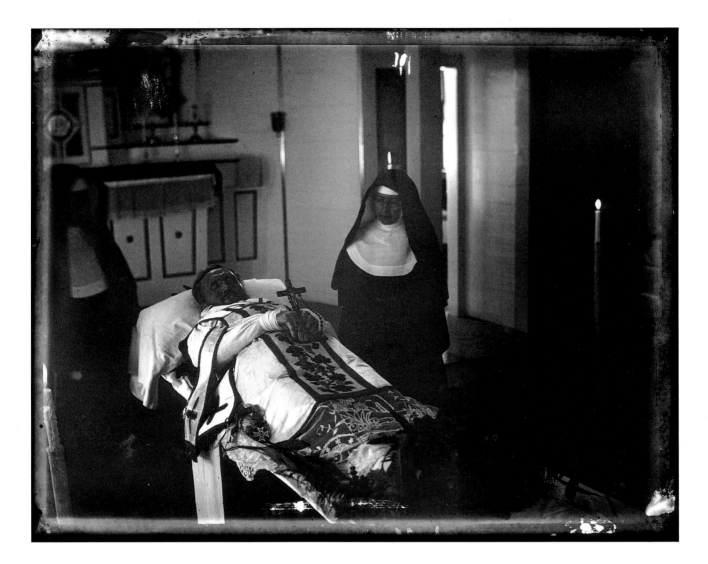

Father Damien lying in state at St. Philomena Church with Mother Marianne Cope (right) and Sister Leopoldina Burns in attendance, Kalawao, 15 April 1889. Sidney Bourne Swift, M.D. Collection of the Damien Museum.

Interior of St. Philomena Church, Kalawao, c. 1890. Sidney Bourne Swift, M.D. Collection of the Damien Museum.

THE EARLY TWENTIETH CENTURY witnessed major changes at Kalaupapa as the philosophy of treatment practiced by Father Damien, Mother Marianne, and their colleagues was applied to the settlement as a whole. This new era in the settlement's history began in 1902, with the arrival of John McVeigh and Dr. William Goodhue, McVeigh to serve as superintendent and Goodhue as resident physician. Both brought to their jobs a firm respect for the people under their care and an understanding that good morale, coupled with a few minor surgical procedures, could not only prolong the patients' lives but also help make those lives worth living. Rather than running a facility where people did little more than wait to die, McVeigh and Goodhue gave Kalaupapa residents the chance to live relatively complete and happy lives despite their affliction.

In the twenty-three years they worked at Kalaupapa, McVeigh and Goodhue turned the settlement into what many regarded as the best leprosy treatment facility in the world. A major building program was undertaken, and activities of all sorts were encouraged. When Jack London visited the settlement in 1907, he observed a Fourth of July celebration that included horse and donkey races, a *luau* (feast), and even a parade. Inspired by his visit, London later described the scene for his readers and concluded that the chief horror of leprosy lay in the minds of those who had never seen a patient and knew nothing about the disease.[12]

While McVeigh, Goodhue, and others made very real efforts to treat leprosy like any other disease and to relate to people with leprosy as human beings with needs equivalent to those of the general population, at the same time it became apparent that the segregation laws were not working and that leprosy was not under control. The issue remained extremely political, with the Board of Health continually at the mercy of the Territorial Legislature for appropriations and thus subject to the whims and demands of legislators, who were capable of exploiting the highly charged issue for their own advancement.

In an attempt to reduce the dependence on local government, the Board of Health, strongly led by its president, Dr. Charles Cooper, devised a plan to interest federal authorities in the islands' leprosy problem. As a result of their initiative, U.S. president Theodore Roosevelt recommended construction in Hawai'i of a hospital and laboratory for the study of leprosy, and on March 3, 1905, Congress passed legislation appropriating $100,000 for these facilities and $50,000 for operations during their first year. This legislation was historic, for it was the first time that Congress authorized a hospital for research on a specific disease.

The Territory turned over a square mile of land at Kalawao to the U.S. Public Health

Kalaupapa Settlement, with view of Kanaana Protestant Church (center), c. 1895.
Unidentified photographer. Collection of Bishop Museum.

and Marine Hospital Service, to be used as the site of the U.S. Leprosy Investigation Station. Dr. Walter Brinckerhoff, a young pathologist from Harvard, was appointed director at the then considerable salary of $5,000 a year, and no expense was spared in constructing the research station. A complex of modern buildings surrounded by a double fence, Brinckerhoff's facility was a veritable fortress against germs. A ten-foot buffer zone between the fences guarded against direct contact with patients outside, and no dogs or birds were allowed. When the station officially opened with nine patients on December 23, 1909, it was a momentous occasion filled with great hope.

Sadly, Dr. Brinckerhoff's extreme caution in designing the station doomed it to failure. The quarantine conditions that he created there would have been admired and understood in Boston, but in Hawai'i, and especially at the settlement, they were completely out of place. The settlement as a whole was already isolated, and the new federal hospital separated its patients, both physically and culturally, even farther than before from the life to

John D. McVeigh, luna nui *(superintendent) of Kalaupapa from 1902–1925, standing outside his quarters on Staff Row, date unknown. Unidentified photographer. Collection of the Hawaiʻi State Department of Health.*

which they were accustomed. It was a *haole* world where one had to eat *haole* food and abide by *haole* rules. It was run by *haole* scientists who seemed more interested in germs than in people and who, despite their fine buildings and fancy equipment, had no cure for leprosy. It is no wonder that the station attracted only the original nine patients and that even they did not stay very long.

The federal government's attempts to conduct research in Hawaiʻi were, however, not a total failure. Although the hospital at Kalawao was unsuccessful, a great deal of valuable research was performed in Honolulu at the U.S. Leprosy Investigation Station at Kalihi Hospital, which had closed in 1875 and re-opened in 1889. In the first two decades of the twentieth century, a number of distinguished scientists were drawn to this institution, where they conducted important studies in epidemiology, methods of transmission, treatment, and cultivation of the leprosy bacillus on artificial media.

Dr. William J. Goodhue (seated), resident physician at the settlement from 1902–1925, with patients he trained to serve as nurses and medical assistants, Kalaupapa, c. 1910. Unidentified photographer. Collection of A. Law.

Dr. Goodhue, the pioneer of leprosy surgery, is a hero who should receive every medal that every individual and every country has ever awarded for courage and life-saving.

                Jack London, "Our Guiltless Scapegoats.
                The Stricken of Molokai,"
                Honolulu Star-Bulletin, 2 June 1916

Baldwin Home for Boys (foreground) and the U.S. Leprosy Investigation Station at Kalawao, completed in 1909. Unidentified photographer. Collection of A. Law.

By far, the most significant work that emanated from the Investigation Station at Kalihi was the development by 1919 of an improved form of chaulmoogra oil, whose curative properties had long been known in Asia. Derived from the seeds of three species of trees, *Hydnocarpus wightiana* (found in southwest India), *Hydnocarpus anthelmintica* (found in Thailand and Indochina), and *Hydnocarpus kurzii* (found in Burma and Assam), chaulmoogra oil was administered orally or by injection, with some patients going so far as to rub it on their skin.

For the first time in the history of leprosy in Hawai'i, physicians and patients alike felt that there was, at last, a cure for the disease. Many people afflicted with leprosy came out of hiding to receive chaulmoogra treatments at Kalihi, and no new patients were sent to Kalaupapa for four years. By 1923, however, the Kalihi Hospital was overflowing with advanced cases, cases that did not appear to respond to the chaulmoogra oil. Faith in its efficacy began to wane, transferrals to the settlement resumed, and by the late 1920s, leprosy was again regarded as incurable.

The early 1930s were, as one Kalaupapa resident recalls, "the dark age of leprosy."[13] Whereas in the early 1920s there had been talk of abandoning the settlement, in 1932 it was almost entirely rebuilt. The physical improvements to the buildings were needed and appreciated, but at the same time, they signaled to the patients that there was little chance they would ever be able to leave. Some Kalaupapa residents recall that during this time they rarely thought about the future because they did not know if they would live out the week. Funerals were held nearly every day, serving as constant reminders that they might be next.

Discovery of the sulfone drugs as a cure for leprosy in the early 1940s and their introduction to Hawai'i in 1946 heralded another era of hope for patients at the settlement, and this time the promise was real. The new medication brought physical changes practically overnight, and as their health improved, patients were increasingly able to participate in sports and other activities. Although the sulfone drugs helped Kalaupapa residents regain a sense of well-being, they received constant reminders that they were still patients and would always be patients in the minds of many. Their outgoing mail was fumigated well into the 1960s, despite a general acknowledgment that fumigation was useless. Like some of the other practices maintained at the settlement, this had the purpose of making the public feel safe, with little consideration given to how it made the patients feel.

The settlement was filled with physical barriers between patients and non-patients. At the visitors' quarters, fences separated patients from their friends and family members;

Brother Aloysius Leisen, known as "Brother Louis," dressing a patient's sores in the Baldwin Home infirmary, Kalaupapa, c. 1920. Unidentified photographer. Collection of the Damien Museum. Brother Louis arrived in 1898 and worked at the Baldwin Home for much of the next forty years.

rows of potted plants divided patients from non-patients on the dance floor; and a multitude of rules and regulations prevented contact between patients and non-patients after working hours. Some of the physical barriers were removed in the late 1940s, largely through the efforts of settlement administrator Lawrence Judd, a former governor of the Territory. Even after many of the overt barriers were dismantled, however, psychological barriers remained. Rules and regulations persisted long after the sulfone drugs had freed the people of Kalaupapa of viable bacilli, reminding them that they were patients and often making them feel less than human.

In 1949, the Territorial government attempted to spark new and enlightened public attitudes toward leprosy in Hawai'i. The legislature decreed that henceforth the official designation for the disease in Hawai'i would be "Hansen's Disease" rather than "leprosy."

The legislature swung back and forth on this issue in ensuing years, but today "Hansen's Disease" is the name mandated for use by government bodies in Hawai'i and the rest of the United States. Elsewhere in the world, the original name is widely employed, and this point of terminology is still hotly debated, but experts in the field all agree that the term "leper" is derogatory and should never be used.

Of greater significance than the shift in nomenclature was a concurrent decision to establish Hale Mōhalu Hospital in Pearl City as an alternative to Kalaupapa for those who wished to leave the settlement and regain their place in the community. Emphasis was to be placed on rehabilitation rather than simply custodial care, and no further patients were to be sent to Kalaupapa unless they expressed an explicit desire to live there. As a consequence, only thirty-two people were admitted to Kalaupapa between 1949 and 1969. It was too early to think about it, but this fact ensured that the settlement would, indeed, come to an end.

These decisions had positive results, but long-held biases and institutional practices die slowly. In 1968, a Committee on Leprosy was established by the Department of Health to review and evaluate the state's program. Acting on an initial recommendation of this committee, the legislature passed a bill that once again made "leprosy" the sanctioned term in Hawai'i, for it was felt that the public could be educated about the disease more readily under its original name than under one that was unfamiliar. This logic still holds, and it is the primary reason that the original term is often used in this essay and in other public discourse.

In 1969, the Committee on Leprosy filed its report, which concluded that the islands' isolation policies were obsolete. The advent of sulfone therapy in the 1940s had rendered people afflicted with leprosy non-infectious and made continued segregation unwarranted. Front-page headlines in the *Honolulu Star-Bulletin* proclaimed: "Leprosy patients are given promise of a new way of life." An editorial the same day commented, "The leprosy patient should from this day forward be nothing more than an average citizen with a disease that needs medical treatment and possibly a brief hospitalization. But he should no longer be an outcast, no longer a leper, no longer a scourge. His life should be no more abnormal than that of any other pill-taker."[14]

This was optimistic thinking. After the legislature acted on the Committee's recommendations, it was true that patients were no longer isolated, and medically the disease was under control, but in other respects things were not so simple. There was still the pervasive Biblical notion of leprosy as a scourge visited upon sinners, and the powerful

The "longhouse" or "caller house" in the visitors' quarters, where patients spoke with family and friends through the chain link fence, Kalaupapa, 1932. Unidentified photographer. Collection of the Hawai'i State Department of Health.

Up until 1969, life in Kalaupapa was a very divided thing. Everything was patients on one side, non-patients on the other side. This area was assigned to *ma'i pake*, as we called ourselves, and [the other] to *kokuas*, who were the non-patients.

> Paul [surname withheld at his request]
> Kalaupapa resident since 1945

Restrooms at Siloama Church with signs reflecting past separation of patients and non-patients, Kalawao, 1984.

Elroy Malo speaking at the first annual meeting of Hui Hoa Aloha, the Hawai'i Hansen's Disease Association, 1986.

When I decided to leave Hale Mōhalu in 1972, psychologically I was prepared never to look back. Since no blind person had ever left the hospital, it was almost like opening a Christmas package because everything was new, everything was so fantastic. In my own mind, I left Hale Mōhalu, got married, and started school full time all on the same weekend. . . . I stumble a lot, and it's nice to have a helping hand now and then, but the fact that I've had the opportunity to do my own thing—that's the main thing.

> Elroy Malo, who lived at the settlement
> and Hale Mōhalu for twenty-five years

stigma associated with the disease made it difficult for a person who contracted it to live the life of "any other pill-taker."

The 1970s and early 1980s were difficult years for the patients and the Department of Health, for it was a time of great transition. Both struggled to deal with the change in laws and attempted to destigmatize the disease. Movies, television shows, and books continued to exploit leprosy for sensational effect. Comedians even told jokes about the disease. Persistent references to "lepers" in the media and elsewhere led the state legislature in 1981 once again to declare "Hansen's Disease" the official term in Hawai'i.

New laws prompted by the findings of the Committee on Leprosy had cleared the way for major changes in the treatment of the disease, but these changes were not universally understood or accepted. The abolition of the isolation policy in 1969 led to the closing of Hale Mōhalu, long regarded by the people of Kalaupapa as their home away from home. Some of its residents were transferred to a ward at Leahi Hospital near Diamond Head, but most were turned out into the community.

This move began as an enlightened response to the new laws but, for a number of reasons, was not entirely successful, and it became a vehicle for expression and discussion of the patients' right to self-determination. At the forefront of this effort were Bernard Punikai'a, Clarence Naia, and Frank Duarte, who continued living at Hale Mōhalu for several years after it was closed. No longer did they or others from Kalaupapa want to be pushed around by the authorities and treated as children. They wanted and demanded a say in their future.

In the mid-1980s, improved communication and cooperation between state officials, Kalaupapa residents, and members of the general public resulted in resolution of the Hale Mōhalu issue. In 1984, public and private organizations joined interested individuals in forming a Coalition for Specialized Housing under the umbrella of the Hawai'i Council of Churches. Working with officials from the Department of Health and other state agencies, the Coalition developed a proposal for an affordable housing complex serving senior citizens and persons with disabilities, including Hansen's Disease patients who wish to regain their place in the community. On May 27, 1988, the Coalition was awarded a lease for part of the old Hale Mōhalu site for this innovative housing project. The agreement reflected concern and commitment on the part of Governor John Waihee and Dr. John Lewin, director of the Department of Health, and indicates the emergence in the islands of a new spirit of understanding and respect for people with Hansen's Disease.

Olivia Breitha with a photograph taken of her on "shipment day," the day she was sent to the settlement, at her home in Kalaupapa, 1985.

How would you feel if somebody told you that treatment would no longer benefit you, coming to this end-of-the-world place when you were nineteen or twenty? You thought, "Oh my god, I'm going there to die, without my family or anybody."

Olivia Breitha, Kalaupapa resident since 1937

Current Realities and Future Challenges

In a society largely ignorant of the realities of leprosy, both health authorities and those who have the disease are faced continually with the task of dispelling myths so that decision makers and the general public can understand the realities of the current situation. It is now known that leprosy is one of the least communicable of all infectious diseases and, in fact, that only about five percent of the world's population is even susceptible to it. Sulfone drugs render the most contagious patient non-infectious after a few days or weeks of treatment, so all new cases are treated on an outpatient basis. Families need never be separated.

Although controllable medically, leprosy is not a disease of the past. Currently there are an estimated eleven million cases worldwide, which means that approximately one in every five hundred people is afflicted with the disease. Difficulties in controlling leprosy stem from the problems of delivering drugs and medical services effectively in developing countries, but it is generally agreed that the biggest barrier to eradication of the disease is the strong social stigma still associated with it. Even in Hawai'i, people who contract leprosy sometimes feel ashamed and are reluctant to come forth for treatment.

Hawai'i is in a unique position to challenge the stigma associated with leprosy, for the islands have not only a moving history to tell but also individuals who are willing to speak out and share their experiences with the disease in an effort to dispel the myths that surround it. Their involvement in educating the public helps people understand the disease in terms of human beings rather than statistics. By expressing the personal impact of the disease, they "put a face on it," which brings it closer to home. They show us the importance of making a distinction between a disease and the people who have it and help us recognize that it is the disease that is fearsome, not those afflicted with it. If society can learn to make this distinction, no one will have to be regarded as a hopeless case. Even though we may not always have a cure for a disease, we can always treat the person who has it with compassion and dignity.

Looking at Kalaupapa today, one sees deteriorating buildings and an aging population. The deterioration of the buildings is a triumph of sorts, for it signals the end of a tragic chapter in the history of Hawai'i. We are coming to the end of Kalaupapa as a leprosy settlement and seeing it evolve into a national historical park where the lessons and memories of the past will be preserved. However, that triumph is marred by the fact that, more than forty years after the introduction of the sulfone drugs and twenty years after the abolition of the isolation laws, there are still patients at Kalaupapa. The fact that they remain provides an indication of how deep the scars of isolation go. Long after the disease became controllable medically, society has yet to deal adequately with the scars resulting from its treatment of the victims. Kalaupapa's history teaches us that it is important to keep in mind the potential social effects of any medical decision, for they will persist long after the disease itself is under control.

Anwei Skinsnes Law

Notes

1. Information on the history of leprosy in Hawai'i has been compiled from original research conducted by the author in preparing her manuscript *A Land Set Apart: Leprosy's Impact on Hawaii and Its Significance for the World*. This information is drawn from a variety of original sources, including Board of Health correspondence, reports and other documents located in the Hawai'i State Archives, the Archives of the Sisters of St. Francis of Syracuse, the State Historical Society of Wisconsin, the Archives of the University of Notre Dame, and other archival and private collections.

2. Ethel M. Damon, *Siloama, the Church of the Healing Spring; the Story of Certain Almost Forgotten Protestant Churches* (Honolulu: Hawaiian Board of Missions, 1948), 12.

3. Gavan Daws, *Holy Man: Father Damien of Molokai* (New York: Harper & Row, 1973), 73.

4. "Statement on Leprosy and Resolutions Adopted by the Hawaiian Evangelical Association, Honolulu, June 10, 1873," *Pacific Commercial Advertiser*, 14 June 1873.

5. Charles Warren Stoddard, *The Lepers of Molokai*, enlarged edition (Notre Dame, Indiana: The Ave Maria Press, 1893), 38.

6. Between closing of the Kalihi Hospital in 1875 and opening of the Kaka'ako Branch Hospital in 1881, patients were simply housed in a detention station adjacent to police headquarters.

7. Robert Louis Stevenson, "To Reverend Sister Marianne," 22 May 1889, Archives of the Sisters of St. Francis of Syracuse.

8. Charles J. Dutton, *The Samaritans of Molokai* (New York: Dodd, Mead & Co., 1932), 198.

9. Joseph Dutton to Elizabeth Harper, 26 July 1889, Archives of the University of Notre Dame.

10. Vital Jourdan, SS.CC., *The Heart of Father Damien*, trans. Francis Larkin, SS.CC., and Charles Davenport (Milwaukee: Bruce Publishing Co., 1955), 374.

11. Joseph Dutton to Elizabeth Harper, 26 July 1889, Archives of the University of Notre Dame.

12. Jack London, "The Lepers of Molokai," *The Contemporary Review* 95, no. 519 (March 1909), 288–97.

13. Olivia Robello Breitha, *Olivia: My Life of Exile in Kalaupapa* (Honolulu: Arizona Memorial Museum Association, 1988), 76.

14. "An Editorial," *Honolulu Star-Bulletin*, 21 March 1969.

They were strangers to each other, collected by common calamity, disfigured, mortally sick, banished without sin from home and friends. Few would understand the principle on which they were thus forfeited in all that makes life dear; many must have conceived their ostracism to be grounded in malevolent caprice; all came with sorrow at heart, many with despair and rage. In the chronicle of man there is perhaps no more melancholy landing than this. . . .

Robert Louis Stevenson
Travels in Hawaii

Kalaupapa ✛ *A Portrait*

You will know that on account of the prevalence of this disease of leprosy in the nation, a division of land has been set apart for the isolation of those affecting [sic]. This measure is for the good of the nation, and being a law, it must be executed. But it is a sad thing to be thus separated from friends and loved ones; how else however are the laws to be executed?

King Lunalilo to residents at Kalawao,
Pacific Commercial Advertiser,
10 May 1873

Up to A.D. 1878, the sick residents of the settlement were simply herded and fed at Kalawao, not provided such necessities as lamp-light, soap and [dressing for their sores], without any means of transportation of their staple article of food which had to be carried by individuals on foot for many miles, and were during all the time, previous to that period, entirely without any medical attendance whatever.

Walter Murray Gibson, "Report of the President of the Board of Health to the Legislative Assembly, 1884" from Leprosy in Hawaii

The north shore of Moloka'i viewed from Kalawao, 1985.

Pavillion at Kalaupapa after a rain, 1984.

Kalaupapa town with St. Francis Church on the left, 1986.

To see where Damien was originally buried, to see the patients that still live here, some of them for as long as sixty years, and to know what's happened here—you start to understand how important this disease is to Hawai'i and society in general and how much effort we have to make to overcome the terrible things that happened . . . as recently as fifty years ago in Hawai'i.

Ronald Metler, M.D.
Hawai'i State Department of Health

When I first came here, I think there was a funeral every day. Of course I didn't know these people because I'd just come, but I guess it told me that it wouldn't be long before I became one of the victims.

Paul [surname withheld at his request]
Resident of Kalaupapa since 1945

Kalaupapa has been nice to us. It's a beautiful spot. Once it was called "The Land of the Living Dead," but today it's called paradise. You can walk around and not get harassed. You can drive your car all year and you don't have to get a license plate. No policeman will tag you with your old license plate. Everybody's friendly here, but the community's getting smaller.

William Malakaua
Kalaupapa resident since 1944

One of many graveyards lining the western shore of Kalaupapa, 1985.

Looking toward Kauhako Crater (its summit marked with a cross) from a graveyard, Kalaupapa, 1985.

A pre-settlement Hawaiian burial site on Kauhako Crater, Kalaupapa, 1984.

"Damien's graveyard" as seen from a window of St. Philomena Church, Kalawao, 1985.

St. Philomena Church viewed from the west, Kalawao, 1985.

Suppose the disease does get my body, God will give me another one on Resurrection Day.

Father Damien, quoted in Vital Jourdan,
The Heart of Father Damien

I myself have been chosen by Divine Providence as a victim to this loathsome disease. I hope to be eternally thankful to God for this favour; as it seems to me that this disease may shorten a little, and even make more direct, my road to our dear fatherland.

Father Damien, in a letter dated 9 November 1887,
from The Life and Letters of Father Damien:
The Apostle of Molokai

The political and journalistic world can boast of very few heroes who compare with Father Damien of Molokai. . . . It is worthwhile to look for the source of such heroism.

Mahatma Gandhi, quoted in M. S. Mehendale,
Gandhi Looks at Leprosy

Father Damien's grave, Kalawao, 1986. At the request of the Belgian government, in 1936 Father Damien's body was exhumed and returned to his homeland, but his presence is still strongly felt in the community, especially on Damien Day, which is usually held on April 15, the anniversary of his death.

Grave of Mother Marianne Cope, Kalaupapa, 1984.

What little good we can do in the world to help and comfort the suffering, we wish to do it quietly and so far as possible, unnoticed and unknown.

Mother Marianne, letter to Lorrin Thurston,
25 May 1888 [Hawaiʻi State Archives]

Mother Marianne Library, Kalaupapa, 1984.

Siloama, "The Church of the Healing Spring," Kalawao, 1986.

I have read and I have heard many stories of Kalaupapa that say the people who lived here, the patients, were bad; that the land was without law and the people were lawless, immoral, engaging in wickedness. But I don't think—in fact, I don't *believe*—that all the people were bad. If this was true, there would not be a church called Siloama, which was the *first* church at Kalawao. I, being a patient, can just imagine how they felt, being taken away, cut off from family, home, friends, and church. What else did they have left except that one refuge, God?

Helen Keao, Kalaupapa resident since 1942

Settlement residents, possibly preparing for a wedding, Kalawao, c. 1915. Unidentified photographer.
Collection of A. Law.

What will leprosy do to my people?/ What will become of our land?
              "Song of the Chanter Kaʻehu,"
                from Mary Kawena Pukui and Alfons Korn,
                  The Echo of Our Song

As for the girls in the Bishop Home, of the many beautiful things I have been privileged to see in life, they, and what has been done for them, are not the least beautiful. . . . The dormitories were airy, the beds neatly made; at every bed-head was a trophy of Christmas cards, pictures and photographs, some framed with shells, and all arranged with care and taste. In many of the beds, besides, a doll lay pillowed.

Robert Louis Stevenson, quoted in Graham Balfour,
The Life of Robert Louis Stevenson

Interior of the Bishop Home, Kalaupapa, c. 1904. Unidentified photographer.
Collection of the Damien Museum.

Abandoned quarters at the Bishop Home, Kalaupapa, 1985. Once filled with young girls and women, today the Bishop Home is occupied by just four Sisters of St. Francis and two other residents.

The social hall at McVeigh Home seen from an abandoned building, Kalaupapa, 1984.

Kitchen in an abandoned house, Kalaupapa, 1985.

Bayview Home, which traditionally housed elderly and blind residents of the settlement, seen from the pool hall, Kalaupapa, 1986.

The old timers used to line the walkway of Bayview Home in the afternoon. They were often the worst cases. Half were blind. The ones who could see would give the others a running description, in Hawaiian, of everything they were seeing.

          Helen Keao, a resident of the settlement since 1942

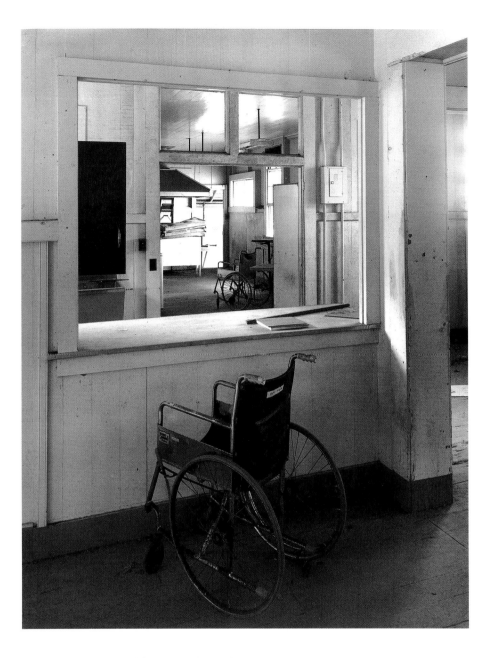

Abandoned kitchen and dining room complex, Bayview Home, Kalaupapa, 1986.

I used to come down to Bayview Home to visit the old people. . . .
They didn't gossip, they talked story. They told me about the old days,
like the time Father Damien's body was taken [back to Belgium]. They
were all sitting on the stone wall, watching, and a lot of them didn't
like that they took Father Damien. . . . They said that was a sad day
for them.

Hyman Fujinaga, Kalaupapa resident since 1942

Operating room in now abandoned Kalaupapa Hospital, 1985.

I worked in the hospital. They had fifty-two inside the big hospital, fifty-two patients. Some were heavy cases, and every day somebody *make* [died], sometimes two. So many people were sick. We had five doctors. I got twenty cents an hour.

Leon Nono, Kalaupapa resident since 1941

Artificial limb in an abandoned house, Kalaupapa, 1986.

Physical impairment, whatever form it takes, can be devastating.
Loss of an eye or eyesight, toes, fingers or limbs—it's always total.
Each of us is a whole person, and replacements to the body are
artificial. We are thus limited, even after therapy.

Henry Nalaielua, Kalaupapa resident since 1941

Richard Marks with his large collection of settlement artifacts, Kalaupapa, 1985. The spoon he is holding was designed for a person whose disabilities made it impossible to grip the handle of a regular spoon.

People were so desperate. That's something you've got to remember. They were so desperate they tried anything. If one thing didn't work, they tried another. This one [indicating a medicine bottle] was called Sanford's Radical Cure, whatever that was. Of course it was probably more opium and alcohol than anything else. . . . This old Scott's Emulsion was pretty popular stateside as well as in Hawai'i. My grandfather used to run a store on Maui, and once asked a [salesman] what this Dr. Kilmer's medication was good for. The guy looked at him for a while and said, "About a million and a half a year." That's the only claim they ever made.

Richard Marks, Kalaupapa resident and
owner-operator of Damien Tours

I have met up with some visitors who, as soon as they got into the van, would say, "Where are the lepers?" I've tried my best to explain to them in a nice way that we're not called "lepers" any more but that we would accept the term "Hansen's Disease." Many of the patients don't mind it if we use the word "leprosy," but to be called a "leper" — many of us don't feel so good when we hear that word.

Helen Keao, Kalaupapa resident since 1942

Helen Keao (left) and Sarah Benjamin at "the grotto," an old outdoor shrine on the grounds of the second Baldwin Home, Kalaupapa, 1986.

Laurenzio Costales (left) and Henry Nalaielua on the porch of the staff dining room, Kalaupapa, 1986.

It's a great feeling to know that you can come into one of those places
where you were never allowed before. I don't ask the reason, I just
like the change. I think if there's any reason for things opening up,
it's because we now have people who have become understanding.
They don't have the fear that people once had about "leprosy," and
they can accept you for what you *are*, not what you *have*.

              Henry Nalaielua, Kalaupapa resident since 1941

Kenso Seki gives John Cambra a haircut with Herbert Hayase looking on, Kalaupapa, 1986.

Frank Duarte at Kalawao, 1985.

In 1958 when I first got discharged, I went to Maui to visit my family.
While I was in Maui, people would look at me, and I would get
self-conscious, guilty. I wanted to come home. I went with my
sister-in-law to a flower shop. She introduced me to a lady, and this is
what the lady said: "Do they let that kind of people out? Don't they
know it's a big mistake to let that kind of people out?"

Frank Duarte, Kalaupapa resident since 1942

Herbert Hayase on the porch of his residence at McVeigh Home, Kalaupapa, 1984.

I'll tell you how cruel some people can be. There was a Japanese storekeeper on Maui who was telling people that my nose and ears were all gone [due to leprosy]. I heard that, so when I went back to Maui, I deliberately passed right in front of his store and showed myself. I was like now, clean. I could see that they were staring at me to find out what was really wrong with me, and nothing was wrong with me. So, you see, a person like that, who has no conscience, makes it hard for us to go outside and live. The majority are okay, but there are a few people who really are not civilized yet.

                    Herbert Hayase, Kalaupapa resident since 1938

Kalaupapa resident John Kaona crafting dolphin pendants from seedpods of the sandbox tree, Kalaupapa, 1986. After National Geographic *published a photograph of him and his jewelry in 1981, many tourists sought out his work.*

If you put your heart into your work, that's the main thing.
John Kaona, speaking shortly before his death in 1988

William Malakaua in his workshop with a photograph of himself in earlier years,
Kalaupapa, 1986.

A lot of our people here, they really amaze you with what they can
do, even with their handicaps. They improvise and help themselves.
Other people would just sit back and let the world go by.

William Malakaua, Kalaupapa resident since 1944

Bernard Punikai'a on the steps of Hale Mōhalu, Pearl City, 1985.

Clarence Naia in front of Kalaupapa Store, 1986.

Hale Mōhalu is one of those special times in our history where we collectively took a stand that was unheard of. We dared to say to the administrators, "No. You may not do with us as you have been doing for the last hundred-plus years."

Bernard Punikai'a
Settlement resident since 1942

What me and Bernard and Frank were doing was fighting for our rights, and we believed in what we were fighting for. That was a sad day when they took us [away from Hale Mōhalu] on the patrol wagon and took us down to the police station. . . . Sometimes there's a picture in me that I'm still there, still on that land. I feel that land still belongs to the patients. Don't belong to nobody else.

> *Clarence Naia*
> *Resident of the settlement since 1954,*
> *speaking before the Hale Mōhalu issue was resolved*

Henry Nalaielua with some of his paintings, Kalaupapa, 1987.

I would say that about ninety-nine percent of the people that I've met
from different walks of life from all over the globe are really curious
[about the settlement]. They want to know what this is all about,
what patients look like, what's going to become of this place, *why* I
am here. . . . I really believe that people need to be educated.

Henry Nalaielua, artist, musician, and past
president of the Kalaupapa Historical Society

Daniel Hashimoto at his vegetable garden, Kalaupapa, 1986.

I was taken away from my parents and raised by my grandmother. I could not get in touch with my dad, no matter how much I tried. I was not allowed to. I never met my father until 1972, when I came to Kalaupapa. When we met one another for the first time, it was like we'd been together from the time I was born. There was love the minute we met.

Pauline Cooke, referring to the past practice at Kalaupapa of removing infants from their parents shortly after birth

Clarence Naia and his daughter Pauline Cooke at his house, Kalaupapa, 1985.

Mariano Rea in Rea's Store, a bar he owns and operates, Kalaupapa, 1985.

Since I'm single, have a pension, and own this business, my nephews and nieces have asked me to help them go to school. I said okay, I was willing to help. From that time until now, I've helped thirteen finish college. Some are in very good positions in the Philippines. Some are in the military, others are pharmacists, agriculturalists, social workers, and teachers.

Mariano Rea, resident of Kalaupapa since 1937

Kenso Seki with pennants collected in the course of his world travels, Kalaupapa, 1986.

We used to go to Honolulu quite a bit. When we went, we saw people turning around to look at us. Gee, that gives you a funny feeling. But then you notice quite a few handicapped people, and it's natural for everybody to look at what they're doing, how they manage. After that, I made up my mind that if they want to look at me, go ahead. Nothing's going to bother me.

                    Kenso Seki, Kalaupapa resident since 1928

Norbert Palea, one of the settlement's youngest residents, outside his newly refurbished house, Kalaupapa, 1986.

Resident Gloria Marks feeding her dogs, Kalaupapa, 1987.

Every night when I go to bed, I always say my prayers. I ask God, my companion and co-pilot, to please protect me and make me a better man . . . make me to like everybody, not hate anybody.

John Cambra, who came to the settlement as a teenager in 1924

John Cambra after sixty years at Kalaupapa, 1984.

Bernard Punikai'a singing "Ave Maria" at the wedding of Henry Law and Anwei Skinsnes in St. Philomena Church, Kalawao, 4 July 1985.

I never had any idea of leaving the settlement. To leave the settlement, no. I feel that we are all alike, and there's nothing to be ashamed of. Today people ask me, "You don't have ideas to leave the settlement?" For what?

Alice Kamaka, Kalaupapa resident since 1919

Alice Kamaka, who has lived at the settlement longer than any surviving resident, Kalaupapa, 1984.

Beach house belonging to Mariano Rea, Kalaupapa, 1986.

Kenso Seki with his still driveable Model-A Ford, Kalaupapa, 1984.

Daniel Hashimoto, pausing as he delivers the community's mail and newspapers, Kalaupapa, 1985.

John Cambra's beach house, Kalaupapa, 1985.

If you want to have good neighbors, go for the dead ones. They don't
bother anything, and they don't talk too much.

John Cambra, Kalaupapa resident since 1924

On the shores of Kalaupapa
We stand with heads bent low;
Shut away by high barrier cliffs,
We recall our own vanished island.

Farewell, farewell, beloved home!
Never shall we see thee more.
Constantly we implore God
To lift this affliction laid upon us.

"Himeni o Kalaupapa,"
from Ethel A. Damon, Siloama

Gravestone, Kalaupapa, 1985.